# Growing in Christ

# Growing in Christ

## by Andrew Murray

GOOD NEWS PUBLISHERS
Westchester, Illinois 60153

GROWING IN CHRIST
A *One Evening Christian Classic* ™
First published in 1979 by
Good News Publishers
Westchester, Illinois 60153.

GROWING IN CHRIST is a new edition,
revised with introductory remarks by Bee Shira,
of the Good News Publishers book GOD'S BEST
SECRETS, an abridgment of the original
Christian classic of the same title.

Library of Congress catalog card number 79-92017
ISBN 0-89107-052-4

# Contents

# 1
# Thou Art the Christ: Responding in Faith and Love

Believing that Jesus is the Christ, the Son of God, is the initial step of faith. But too often we stop here. When He asks, "Believe ye that I am able to do this?" we sometimes hedge and are not as willing to acknowledge that the Christ we trusted for salvation is waiting to work in our lives. In the following selections the author focuses on Christ's life and death, on His power and presence, and on some of His words to lead us into a deeper response of faith and love here and now.

## Believing God

"If thou canst believe, all things are possible to him that believeth. And straightway the father of the child said with tears: Lord, I believe, help Thou mine unbelief" (Mark 9:23, 24). "Jesus said, He that believeth in Me, though he were dead, yet shall he live. Believeth thou this? She saith unto Him, Yea, Lord, I believe" (John 11:25, 26, 27).

To what we have seen and heard of Christ Jesus, our heart is ready to say with Martha, in answer to Christ's question: "Yea, Lord, I have believed that Thou art the Christ, the Son of God." But when it comes to the point of believing that Christ promises to us the power of the resurrection life, and His presence every day, we do not find it so easy to say, "I do believe that this omnipotent, omnipresent, unchangeable Christ, our Redeemer God, will walk with me all the day and give me the unceasing consciousness of His holy presence." It looks too much to venture. And yet it is this faith that Christ asks, and is waiting to work within us.

It is well that we understand clearly what the conditions are on which Christ offers to reveal to us in experience the secret of His abiding presence. God cannot force His blessings on us against our will. He seeks in every possible way to stir our desire, and to help us to realize that He is able and willing to make His promises true. The resurrection of Christ from the dead is His great plea, His all-prevailing argument. If He could raise that dead Christ, Who had died under the burden of all our sin, surely He can fulfill in our hearts His promise that Christ can be our life all the day.

In view of what we have said and seen about Christ as our Lord are we willing to take His word and to rest in the promise: "Lo, I am with you all the day?" Christ's question comes to us: "Believest thou this?" Let us not rest until we have bowed before Him and said: "Yea, Lord, I do believe."

## Taking Up Our Cross

The cross of Christ is His greatest glory. Because He humbled Himself to the death of the cross, therefore God hath highly exalted Him. The cross was the power that conquered Satan and sin.

The Christian shares with Christ in the cross. The crucified Christ lives in him through the Holy Spirit, and the spirit of the cross inspires him. He lives as one who has died with Christ and as he realizes the power of Christ's crucifixion, he lives as one who has died to the world and to sin. The power becomes a reality in his life.

Our Lord said to His disciples: "Take up your cross and follow Me." Did they understand this? They had seen men carrying a cross, and knew that it meant a painful death on the cross. All His life Christ bore His cross—the death sentence that He should die for the world. And each Christian must bear his cross, acknowledging that he is worthy of death, believing that he is crucified with Christ, and that the crucified One lives in him. "Our old man is crucified with Christ." "He that is Christ's hath crucified the flesh with all the lusts thereof." When we have accepted this life of the cross, we will be able to say with Paul: "Far be it from me to glory save in the cross of our Lord Jesus Christ."

This is a deep spiritual truth. Think and pray about it, and the Holy Spirit will teach you. Let the disposition of Christ on the cross—His humility, His sacrifice of all worldly honor, His Spirit of self-denial—take possession of you. The power of His death will work in you, and you will become like Him in His death, and will know Him and the power of His resurrection. Take time that Christ through His Spirit may reveal Himself as the Crucified One.

## Christ Living in Us

In all our study and worship of Christ we find our thoughts gathering round these aspects of our Savior: The incarnate Christ, the crucified Christ, the enthroned Christ, the indwelling Christ, and Christ coming in glory. If the first be the seed, the second is the seed cast into the ground, and the third the seed growing up to heaven. Then follows the fruit through the Holy Spirit, Christ dwelling in the heart; and finally the gathering of the fruit when Christ appears.

Paul tells us that it pleased God to reveal His Son in him. And he gives his testimony resulting from that revelation: "Christ liveth in me" (Gal. 2:20). Of that life he says that its chief mark is that he is crucified with Christ. It is this that enables him to say, "I live no longer"; in Christ he had found the death of self. Just as the cross is the chief characteristic of Christ Himself—"A lamb as it had been slain in the midst of the throne"—so the life of Christ in Paul made him inseparably one with his crucified Lord. So completely was this the case that he could say: "Far be it from me to glory save in the cross of our Lord Jesus Christ, through which I am crucified to the world."

If Christ so actually lived in Paul that he no longer lived, what became of his responsibility? Paul's answer: "I live by the faith of the Son of God, Who loved me and gave Himself for me." His life was every moment a life of faith in Him who had loved him and given Himself so completely that He had undertaken at all times to be the life of His willing disciple.

This was the sum of Paul's teaching. He asks for intercession that he might speak "the mystery of Christ"; "even the riches of the glory of this mystery among the Gentiles, which is Christ in you, the hope of glory" (Col. 2:2; 1:27). The indwelling Christ was the secret of his life of faith, the one power, the one aim of all his life and work, the hope of glory. Let us believe in the abiding presence of Christ as the sure gift to each one who trusts Him fully.

## The All-Powerful Christ

Before Christ gave His disciples their Great Commission to take His Gospel to every creature, He revealed Himself in His divine power as a partner with God, the Almighty One. It was this that enabled the disciples to undertake work in simplicity and boldness. They had begun to know Him in that mighty resurrection power which had conquered sin and death; there was nothing too great for Him to command or for them to undertake.

Every disciple of Jesus Christ who desires to take part in the victory that overcometh the world needs time, and faith, and the Holy Spirit to come under the full conviction that it is as the servant of the omnipotent Lord Jesus that he is to take his part in the work. He is to count literally upon the daily experience of being "strong in the Lord and in the power of His might." The word of promise gives courage to obey implicitly the command.

Just think of what the disciples had learned of the power of Christ Jesus here on earth. And yet that was but little as compared with the greater works that He was now to do in and through them. He has the power to work even in the feeblest of His servants with the strength of Almighty God. He has power to use their apparent impotence to carry out His purposes. He has the power over every enemy and every human heart, over every difficulty and danger.

But let us remember that this power is never meant to be experienced as if it were our own. It is only as Jesus Christ as a living Person dwells and works with His divine energy in our own heart and life that there can be power in our preaching as a personal testimony. It was when Christ had said to Paul, "My strength is made perfect in weakness," that he could say, what he never learned to say before, "When I am weak, then am I strong." The disciple of Christ understands that power has been entrusted to Him, to be received from Him hour by hour.

## The Omnipresent Christ

Man's first thought in his conception of a God is that of power, however limited. In thinking of the true God it is His omnipotence: "I am God Almighty." The second thought in Scripture is His omnipresence. God gave His servants the promise of His unseen presence with them. To His "I am with thee," their faith responded: "Thou art with me."

When Christ had said to His disciples, "All power is given unto Me in heaven and on earth," the promise "I am with you alway" immediately follows, also. The omnipotent One is the omnipresent One.

The revelation of God's omnipresence in the man Christ Jesus makes the mystery still deeper. It also makes the grace that enables us to claim this presence as our strength and our joy even more blessed. And yet how often a servant of Christ finds it difficult to understand how it can become the practical experience of his daily life.

Here, as elsewhere in the spiritual life, everything depends upon faith, accepting Christ's word as a divine reality, and trusting the Holy Spirit to make it true to us from moment to moment. When Christ says "always" (Gr. "all the days"), He means to assure us that there is not a day of our life in which that blessed presence is not with us. And that "all the days" implies "all the day." there need not be a moment in which that presence cannot be our experience. It does not depend upon what we can effect, but upon what He undertakes to do.

The omnipotent Christ is the omnipresent Christ. His presence can be with each of His servants who trusts Him for it.

Our attitude must be that of a quiet, restful faith, of a humble, lowly dependence, in accordance with the word: "Rest in the Lord, and wait patiently for Him."

"Lo, I am with you alway." Let our faith in Christ, the omnipresent One, be in the quiet confidence that He will every day and every moment keep us as the apple of His eye, and in perfect peace, knowing that we can experience all the light and strength we need in His service.

## The Loving Christ

It was to Mary who loved much that Christ first revealed Himself. Then in Peter's first vision of the Lord, in the upper room at Emmaus, in His appearance to the ten, and in revealing Himself to Thomas. It was to the intense devotion of the prepared heart that Christ manifested Himself. And now in manifesting Himself to Peter love is again the keynote.

We can easily understand why Christ asked the question thrice, Lovest thou Me? It was to remind Peter of the self-confidence in which he had said: "Though I should die with Thee, I will not deny Thee"; of the need of heart-searching before he could be sure that his love was true; of the need of deep penitence, and of love for the full restoration to his place in the heart of Jesus. It had to be the first condition for feeding His sheep and caring for His lambs.

God is love. Christ is the Son of His love. Having loved His own, He loved them to the uttermost, and said: "As the Father loved Me, so love I you." He asked that they should prove their love to Him by keeping His commandments and loving each other with the love with which He loved them. In heaven and on earth, in the Father and in the Son, and in us, and in all our work for Him and our care for souls, the greatest thing is love.

To everyone who longs to have Jesus manifest Himself—"I am with you alway"—the essential requisite is love. Peter teaches us that such love is not in the power of man to offer. But such love came to him through the power of Christ's death and His resurrection life, of which Peter became partaker. Thank God, if Peter the self-confident could be so changed, cannot we believe that Christ will work in us the wondrous change too?

## Christ Manifesting Himself

Christ had promised the disciples that the Holy Spirit would come to reveal His presence with them. When the Spirit came, He through the Spirit would manifest Himself to them. They would know Him in a new way, in the power of the Spirit, and have Him more intimately with them than they had known.

The condition of this revelation of Himself is love: "He that keepeth My commandments, he it is that loveth Me: and he that loveth Me shall be loved of My Father, and I will love him." It is to be the meeting of divine and human love. The love with which Christ had loved them had taken possession of their hearts, and would show itself in the love of a full and absolute obedience. The Father would see this, and His love would rest upon the soul; Christ would love him with the special love drawn out by the loving heart, and would manifest Himself. The love of heaven shed abroad in the heart would be met by the new and blessed revelation of Christ Himself.

But this is not all. When the question was asked, "What is it?" the answer came again, "If a man love Me, he will keep My Word"; and then again, "My Father will love him, and We will come unto him and make Our abode with him." In the heart thus prepared by the Holy Spirit, obedient and fully surrendered, the Father and the Son will take up their abode.

And now, nothing less is what Christ promises them: "Lo, I am with you alway." That "with" implies "in"— Christ with the Father, dwelling in the heart by faith. Oh, that everyone would study, and believe, and claim in child-like simplicity the blessed promise: "I will manifest Myself unto him."

## Christ's Love in Us

The Lord gave His disciples a new commandment, that they should love one another, as He had loved them. To this end He wanted them to know the nature of the love He had for them—nothing less than the love wherewith the Father had loved Him. It is the everlasting, unchangeable, divine love with which the Father loved the Son, that the Son loved us, and that we should show one another.

The thought is so heavenly that we need time to grasp it. Pray about it and let God's Spirit make it a blessed reality: the love of God to Christ, the love of Christ to me, my love to the brethren, is one and the same.

God sent His Son to earth to manifest this love. The same love that God had to His Son, He had in His heart for all mankind. This same love Jesus exercised toward His disciples. This love was given them when the Holy Spirit was poured out on the Day of Pentecost, that they

might love one another—even love those who were
enemies of Christ.

It is all one and the same love. Not merely a feeling or
a blessed experience, but a living divine power, flowing
from the Father to the Son, working in the hearts of the
disciples through the Son, and streaming forth to the
whole world.

We say: "We cannot love others as Christ has loved
us." It is not impossible. The Holy Spirit, as the power of
this holy love, sheds it abroad in our hearts. This is
God's own Word. He who meditates on it until he be-
lieves it will have courage to bring his petitions to the
Throne of Grace, and to receive the love which passes
all understanding.

## Rejoicing in God's Presence

"Glad tidings of great joy," the angel called the Gospel
message. The Psalmist called it "the joyful sound." That
blessedness consists in God's people walking in the light
of God, and rejoicing in His name all the day. Undis-
turbed fellowship, never-ending joy, is their portion.
Even in the Old Testament such was at times the experience of the saints. But there was no continuance; the
Old Testament could not secure that. Only the New
Testament offers it.

In every well-ordered family one finds the father de-
lighting in his children, and the children rejoicing in
their father's presence. And this mark of a happy home
on earth is what the Heavenly Father has promised and
delights to work in His people; walking in the light of
His countenance, it has been made possible in Christ
through the Holy Spirit filling the heart with the love of
God. It is the heritage of all who desire to love God with

all their heart and with all their strength.

And yet how many of God's children simply think it impossible and have given up the desire for a life of rejoicing in God's presence. And yet Christ promised it so definitely: "These things have I spoken unto you, that My joy may be in you, and that your joy may be fulfilled." "I will see you again, and your heart shall rejoice, and your joy no one taketh away from you."

Let us think of the Father's longing to have the perfect confidence and love of His children, of the children's need of the Father's presence every moment for their happiness and strength. Think of the power of Christ by the Holy Spirit to maintain this life in us; and be content with nothing less than the blessedness of them that know the joyful sound: "They walk in the light of Thy countenance, and rejoice in Thy Name all the day; for Thou art the glory of their strength."

The deeper we seek to enter into God's will for us, the stronger our faith will be that the Father can be content with nothing less than His child walking in the light of His countenance, and rejoicing in His Name all the day; and the stronger will the assurance come that what the Father has meant for us will be wrought in us through Christ and the Holy Spirit. Let us hold fast the word—all the day.

## Praising God

Praise will ever be a part of Adoration. Adoration, when it has entered God's presence, and had fellowship with Him, will ever lead to the praise of His name. Let praise be a part of the incense we bring before God in our quiet time.

When the children of Israel had been delivered from

the power of Egypt, Moses burst forth in song of praise for their redemption.

"Who is like unto Thee, O Lord, among the gods? Who is like Thee, glorious in holiness, fearful in praises, doing wonders?"

In the Psalms we see what a large place praise ought to have in the spiritual life. There are more than sixty Psalms of praise, becoming more frequent as the Book draws to its close. See Ps. 95-101; 103-107; 111-118; 134-138; 144-150. The last five are Hallelujah psalms, with the word, "Praise ye the Lord," as the beginning and the ending. And the very last repeats, "praise Him" twice in every verse, and ends, "Let everything that hath breath praise the Lord."

Let us take time to study this until our lives are one continual song of praise:

"I will bless the Lord at all times; His praise shall continually be in my mouth." "Every day will I bless Thee." "I will sing praises unto my God while I have my being."

With the coming of Christ into the world, there was a new outburst of praise in the songs of the angels, of Mary, of Zechariah, and of Simeon.

And then we find in the song of Moses and the Lamb (Rev. 15:3) the praise of God filling creation: "Great and marvelous are Thy works, Lord God Almighty. Who shall not fear Thee, O Lord, and glorify Thy Name? for Thou only art holy"; ending (Rev. 19:1-6) with the fourfold "Hallelujah, Amen!" "For the Lord our God, the Almighty, reigneth."

O child of God, let the quiet time with God lead the heart to unceasing praise.

# 2
# Surrendering Self: Learning From Christ's Example

In the hymn we sing "I surrender all." But do we? "All" is so inclusive—and we tend to hold back something, perhaps without even realizing it. Often it is self. Instead of submitting we exalt ourselves. In contrast Christ practiced self-denial, telling the Father, "Not as I will, but as Thou wilt." In these readings we are reminded that surrendering self is not once-for-all: it is a continuing need that Christ help us to deal with if we are willing.

## Surrendering to Christ

In studying the promises Jesus gave to His disciples in the last night, the question comes, What was it that made these men worthy of the high honor of being baptized with the Holy Spirit from heaven? The answer is simple. When Christ called them, they forsook all and followed Him. They denied themselves and obeyed His commands. They followed Him to Calvary, and amid its suffering and death their hearts clung to Him alone. It was this that prepared them for receiving a share in His resurrection life, and so becoming fitted here on earth to be filled with that Spirit, even as He received the fulness of the Spirit from the Father in glory.

Just as Jesus Christ had to sacrifice all to be an offering to God, so all His people, from Abraham and Jacob, and Joseph downward to His twelve disciples, have had to be men who gave up all to follow the Divine leading, and lived separated unto God, that the Divine power could fulfil His purposes through them.

It was thus with Paul too. To count all things but loss for Christ was the keynote of His life, as it must be of ours, if we are to share fully in the power of His resurrection. But how little the Church understands that we have been redeemed from the world, to live wholly and only for God and His love. As the merchantman who found the treasure in the field had to sell all he had to purchase it, Christ claims the whole heart and the whole life and the whole strength, if we are indeed to share with Him in the victory through the power of the Holy Spirit. The law of the kingdom is unchangeable; all things loss for the excellency of the knowledge of Christ Jesus my Lord.

The disciples had to spend years with Christ to be prepared for Pentecost. Christ calls us to walk every day in the closest union with Himself, to abide in Him and to live as those who are not their own. It is in this we shall find the path to the fulness of the Spirit.

Let us boldly believe that such a life is meant for us. Let our heart's fervent desire reach out after nothing less than this. Let us love the lord our God and Christ our Savior with our whole heart. We shall be more than conquerors through Him that loved us.

## Doing It Daily

The death of Christ on the cross is the highest and the holiest that can be known of Him even in the glory of heaven. And the highest and the holiest that the Holy Spirit can work in us is to take us up and to keep us in the fellowship of the cross of Christ. We need to enter deeply into the truth that Christ the beloved Son of the Father could not return to the glory of heaven until He had first given Himself over unto death. As this great truth opens up to us, it will help us to understand how in our life, and in our fellowship with Christ, it is impossible for us to share His life until we have first surrendered ourselves every day to die to sin and to abide in the unbroken fellowship with our crucified Lord.

And it is from Christ alone that we can learn what it means to have fellowship with His sufferings, and to be made conformable unto His death. When in the agony of Gethsemane He looked forward to what a death on the cross would be, He got a vision of what it would mean to die with God's countenance so turned from Him that not a single ray of its light could penetrate the darkness. He prayed that the cup might pass from Him. But when no answer came, and He understood that the Father could not allow the cup to pass, He yielded up His whole will and life in the word: "Thy will be done." O Christian, in this word of the Lord in His agony, you can enter into fellowship with Him, and in His strength your heart will be made strong to believe most confidently that God in His omnipotence will enable you in very deed with Christ to yield up everything, because you have been crucified with Him.

"Thy will be done"; let this be the deepest and the highest word in your life. In the power of Christ with Whom you have been crucified, and in the power of His Spirit, the definite daily surrender to the ever-blessed will of God will become the joy and the strength of your life.

## Denying Self

Christ had for the first time definitely announced that He would have to suffer much and would be killed and raised again. "Peter rebuked him, saying, 'Be it far from Thee, Lord: this shall never be unto Thee.' " Christ's answer was, "Get thee behind Me, Satan." The spirit of Peter, seeking to turn Him away from the cross and its suffering, was nothing but Satan tempting Him to turn aside from what God had appointed as our way of salvation.

Christ then adds the words of our text, in which He uses for the second time the words "take up the cross." Along with them He uses a significant expression revealing what is implied in the cross: "If any man come after Me, let him deny himself, and take up his cross." When Adam sinned, he fell out of the life of Heaven and of God into the life of the world and of self. Self-pleasing, self-sufficiency, self-exaltation, became the law of his life. When Jesus Christ came to restore man to his original place, "being in the form of God, He emptied Himself, taking the form of a servant, and humbled Himself even to the death of the cross." What He has done Himself He asks of all who desire to follow Him: "If any man will come after Me, let him deny himself."

Instead of denying himself, Peter denied his Lord: "I know not the Man." When a man learns to obey Christ's commands, he says of himself: "I know not the man." It is the secret of true discipleship, to bear the cross, to acknowledge the death sentence that has been passed on self, and to deny any right that self has to rule over us.

Death to self is to be the Christian's watchword. The surrender to Christ is to be so entire, to live for those around us so complete, that self is never allowed to come down from the cross to which it has been crucified, but is ever kept in the place of death.

Let us listen to the voice of Jesus: "Deny self;" and ask that by the grace of the Holy Spirit, as the disciples of Christ Who denied Himself for us, we may ever live as those in whom self has been crucified with Christ, and in whom the crucified Christ now lives as Lord and Master.

## Dying to Self

Every inch of our life's road is to be made up of dying to ourselves. To think of anything but the continual total denial of our earthly nature is to overlook the thing on which all depends.

You rejoice in thinking that in knowing these truths you have found the pearl of great price. But notice, it is not yours till you sell all that you have and buy it. Now self is all that you have; you have no good of your own, nothing is yours but this self. Before the pearl is yours you must die to all your possession of self. It is an apostate nature and corrupts everything that it touches. All evil tempers are born and nourished in self. Die to this self, to this inward nature, and outward enemies are overcome.

The ground of all true religion is to overcome that earthly life which overcame Adam in the fall. The Son of God calls us to die to this life and take up His cross. When the human soul turns from itself, and turns to God, dies to itself and lives to God in the Spirit of the holy Jesus, then only is it delivered from covetousness and sensuality, from a worldly spirit, from self-interest and self-exaltation, hatred and envy.

The total dying to self is the only foundation of a solid piety. Thus the spiritual life begins at the true root, grows out of death, and is born in a heart broken off from all its own natural life.

Our blessed Lord Jesus could not be raised from the dead into the glory of the Father's right hand until He had died on the Cross. This is the new and living way which He opened up through the rent veil of the flesh into the Holiest of All. And it is in this new and living way with our flesh also crucified and given over to the death, that we enter into the life and joy of God's presence here upon earth. The continual denial of self is one of the secrets of the continual enjoyment of God's presence and power working in our hearts.

## Having the Mind of Christ

What was the mind that was in Christ Jesus? "Being in the form of God, He emptied Himself, taking the form of a servant, being made in the likeness of men; He humbled Himself, becoming obedient even unto death, yea, the death of the cross." Self-emptying and self-sacrifice, obedience to God's will, and love to men, even unto the death of the cross—such was the character of Christ for which God so highly exalted Him. Such is the character of Christ that we are to imitate. He was made in the likeness of men, that we might be conformed into the likeness of God.

Self-effacement, self-sacrifice, that God's will might be done, and that man might be saved—such was the life of Christ. "Love seeketh not its own." This was His life; He lived only to please God and to bless men.

Let no one say that this is an impossibility. "What is impossible with men is possible with God." We are called to work out this salvation of a Christlike character with fear and trembling; for "it is God that worketh in us both to will and to do of His good pleasure." He of whom Christ said, "it is the Father in Me that doeth the works," is He who works in us to will and to do.

It has been said that "the missionary who is to commend the Gospel must first embody it in a character fully conformed to the likeness of Jesus Christ. It is only as far as he can live Christ before the eyes of the converts that he can help them to understand his message. It has at times come to pass that our representatives on the field, just because they are what we have made them, have far too often hidden the Christ whom they are giving their lives to reveal."

Let us not rest until our faith lays hold of the promise, "It is God that worketh in us." The confidence will be aroused, that as the character of Christ is the revelation with which every missionary has been entrusted, so the power will be given to fulfil this high and holy calling. Let ministers and missionaries and all intercessors make it their great plea and aim to have the mind that was in Christ Jesus.

## Following the Lamb

It may not be easy to say exactly what is implied in this following of the Lamb in the heavenly vision. But we may be sure that it will be the counterpart in glory of what it is to follow in the footsteps of the Lamb here upon earth. As the Lamb on earth reveals what the Lamb in heaven will be, so His followers on earth can show forth something of the glory of what it is to follow Him in heaven.

And how may the footsteps of the Lamb be known? "He humbled Himself." "As a Lamb that is led to the slaughter, He opened not His mouth" (Isa. 53:7). It is

the meekness and gentleness and humility that marked
Him which calls for His followers to walk in His
footsteps.

Our Lord Himself said: "Learn of Me, that I am meek
and lowly of heart, and ye shall find rest unto your
souls." Paul writes: "Have this mind in you, which was
also in Christ Jesus" (Phil. 2:5). And then he teaches us
in what that mind consisted: Being in the form of God,
He emptied Himself; He was made in the likeness of
men; He took the form of a servant; He humbled Himself; He became obedient unto death, even the death of
the cross. The Lamb is our Lord and Lawgiver. He
opened the only path that leads to the throne of God. It
is as we learn from Him what it means to be meek and
lowly, what it means to empty ourselves, to choose the
place of the servant, to humble ourselves and become
obedient, even unto death, the death of the cross, that
we shall find the new and living way that leads us
through the rent veil into the Holiest of All.

"Wherefore also God highly exalted Him, and gave
unto Him the name which is above every name" (Phil.
2:9). It is because Christians so little bear the mark of
this self-emptying and humiliation unto death, that the
world refuses to believe in the possiblity of a Christ-
filled life.

Children of God, study the Lamb who is to be your
model and your Savior. Let Paul's words be the keynote
of your life: "I have been crucified with Christ; yet I
live; and yet no longer I, but Christ liveth in me." Here
you have the way to follow the Lamb even to the glory of
the Throne of God in Heaven.

# 3
# Renewal Through Daily Fellowship: Make It a Standing Appointment

Renewal is a word we hear in connection with everything from blighted cities to expiring contracts. Regardless of how it is used, the word carries the idea of making new or restoring. Webster has a special listing—"to make new spiritually." Nowhere is renewal more needed on a regular basis than in the inner man. This section considers God's part and our part in fellowship—the daily dialog that sparks Christian renewal.

## The Necessity of a Daily Walk

There is one lesson that all young Christians should learn—the absolute necessity of fellowship with Jesus each day. This lesson is not always taught at the beginning of the Christian life, nor is it always understood by the young convert. He should realize that forgiveness of sins, his acceptance of God's child, and his joy in the Holy Spirit, can only be preserved by daily renewal in fellowship with Jesus Christ.

Many Christians backslide because this truth is not clearly taught. They are unable to stand against the temptations of the world, or of their old nature. They strive to fight against sin, and to serve God, but they have no strength. They have never really grasped the secret: The Lord Jesus will every day from heaven continue His work in me. But on one condition—the soul must give Him time each day to impart His love and His grace. Time alone with the Lord Jesus each day is the indispensable condition of growth and power.

Read Matthew 11:25-30. Listen to Christ's word: "Come unto Me, and I will give you rest. Learn of Me, and ye shall find rest unto your souls." The Lord will teach us how meek and humble He is. Bow before Him, tell Him that you long for Him and His love, and His love will rest on you. This is a thought not only for young Christians, but for all who love the Lord. This book is to help those who desire to live this life of fellowship with Christ. We will try to put the message as clearly, as lovingly, as urgently as possible. For Christ's sake, and in order to please Him; for my own sake, to enable me to enjoy this blessed experience each day, I will learn the lesson, to spend time each day—without exception—in fellowship with my Lord. So will the inner man be renewed from day to day.

## The Nearness of God

It has been said that the holiness of God is the union of God's infinite distance from sinful man with God's infinite nearness in His redeeming grace. Faith must seek to realize both the distance and the nearness.

In Christ God has come near, so very near to man, and now the command comes: If you want to come still nearer, you must make the move. The promised nearness of Christ Jesus expressed in the promise, "Lo, I am with you alway," can only be experienced as we move near to Him.

That means, at the beginning of each day to yield ourselves for His holy presence to rest upon us. It means a voluntary, intentional, and whole-hearted turning away from the world, to wait for God to reveal Himself. It is impossible to expect the abiding presence of Christ with us through the day, unless there be the definite daily exercise of strong desire and childlike trust in His word: "Draw nigh to God, and He will draw nigh to you."

Further, it means the simple, childlike offering of ourselves and our lives in everything to do His will and to please Him. His promise is sure: "If a man love Me he will keep My words, and My Father will love him, and we will make our abode in him."

Then comes the quiet assurance of faith, even if there is not much feeling or sense of His presence, that God is with us, and that as we go out to do His will He strengthens us in the inner man for the work we do for Him.

Child of God, let these words come to you with a new meaning each morning: "Draw nigh to God, and He will draw nigh to you." Wait patiently, and He will speak in divine power: "Lo, I am with you alway."

## Too Little Faith

The disciples had often cast out devils. But at least once (see Matt. 17:19-21) they had been impotent. They asked the Lord what the reason might be. His answer: "Because of your little faith."

We have here the reply to a question so often asked, How is it that we cannot live that life of unbroken fellowship with Christ which the Scripture promises? Simply, because of our unbelief. We do not realize that faith must accept and expect that God will, by His almighty power, fulfill every promise He has made. We do not live in that utter helplessness and dependence on God alone which is the very essence of faith. We are not strong in faith, fully persuaded that what God has promised He is able and willing to perform. We do not give ourselves with our whole heart, believing that God by His almighty power will work wonders in our hearts.

Why is this faith so often lacking? "Howbeit this kind goeth not out but by prayer and fasting." A strong faith in God results from a life in close touch with Him. We cannot call up faith at our bidding; it needs close intercourse with God. It needs not only prayer, but fasting too in the larger and deeper meaning of that word. It requires doing away with pleasing the flesh and the pride of life which is the essence of a worldly spirit. To gain the prizes of the heavenly life here on earth means to sacrifice what earth offers. Just as this kind of faith needs God to satisfy the human heart, and work His mighty miracles in it, it needs the whole man, utterly given up to God, to have that power which can cast out every evil spirit. Prayer and fasting are essential.

## Submitting Your Timetable

Time is lord of all things. The history of the world is proof of how, slowly but surely, time has made man what he is today. We see it in the growth of the child's to manhood, both physically and mentally, in labors and attainments. It is under the law of time and its inconceivable power that we spend our lives.

This is specially true in religion and intercourse with God. Time here too is master. What fellowship with God! What holiness and blessedness! What likeness to His image, and what power in His service for blessing to men—all on the condition that we have sufficient time with God for His holiness to shine on us, and to make us partakers of His Spirit and His life. The very essence of religion lies in time with God. And yet how many of God's servants who, while giving their lives to His service, frankly confess that the feebleness of their spiritual life as missionaries, and the inadequate results of their work, are due to not taking time for daily communion with God.

What is the cause behind this sad confession? Nothing but a lack of faith in the God-given assurance that time spent alone with God will bring into the lives of His servants the power to enable them to use all their time in His fellowship.

O my brother who complains that overwork, or too much zeal is hindering spiritual efficiency, do you not see that by submitting your timetable to the inspection of Christ and His Holy Spirit, a new life can be yours?

## Dialoging With God

Prayer and the Word of God are inseparable, and should always go together in the quiet time. In His Word God speaks to me; in prayer I speak to God. If there is to be true intercourse, God and I must both take part. If I simply pray, without using God's Word, I am apt to use my own words and thoughts. Taking God's thoughts from His Word, and presenting them before Him gives prayer its power. Then I am enabled to pray according to God's Word. This is indispensable for true prayer!

When I pray, I must know God aright and it is through the Word that the Holy Spirit gives me right thoughts of Him. The Word will also teach me how wretched and sinful I am. It reveals to me the wonders God will do for me, and the strength He will give me to

do His will. The Word teaches me how to pray—with
strong desire, with a firm faith, and with perseverance.
The Word teaches me not only what I am, but what I
may become through God's grace. And above all, it reminds me each day that Christ is the great Intercessor,
allowing me to pray in His Name.

O Christian, learn to renew your strength each day in
God's Word, and so pray according to His will.

Turning to the other side, we need prayer when we
read God's Word—prayer to be taught by God to understand His Word, prayer to rightly know and use
God's Word and prayer that I may see in the Word that
is all in all, and will be all in me.

Blessed is the quiet time, where I may approach God
in Christ through the Word and prayer, offer myself to
God and His service, and be strengthened by the Holy
Spirit to daily walk in this love.

# 4
# Removing Barriers to Fellowship: Confess and He Will Forgive

The Church at Ephesus is a sobering reminder that one barrier between God and believers can cause a breach in fellowship. The zeal of this church had continued, but its love for God had diminished. In this group of writings, Dr. Murray deals with lack of love and such other impediments to fellowship as knowing God too little, failing to confess sin, loving the allurements of the world, and failing to fear God, to yield to Him and to please Him. He calls for the Psalmist's response: "Father, I will seek Thee with all my heart and will."

## Knowing God Better

You may ask: "Why is it that prayer and intercession are not a greater delight? Is there a way in which we may become fitted to make fellowship with God our chief joy, and as intercessors to bring down His power and blessing on those for whom we pray?"

The chief answer is undoubtedly: We know God too little. In our prayer, we are concerned less with His presence than the thing on which our heart is set. We think mostly of ourselves, our need, and weakness, our desire and prayer. But we forget that in every prayer God must be First, must be All. To find Him, to wait in His presence, to be assured that He actually listens to what we say, and is working in us—it is this that gives the inspiration that makes prayer as natural to us as the intercourse of a child with his father.

And how do we attain this fellowship with Him? We must take time to make Himself known to us. Believe with your whole heart, that just as you present yourself to God as a supplicant, so God presents Himself to you as the Hearer of Prayer. It is not the amount or the earnestness of your words in which prayer has its power, but in the living faith that God Himself is taking you and your prayer into His loving heart. He Himself will give the assurance that in His time your prayer will be heard.

The object of this book is to help you to know how to meet God in every prayer. We shall suggest texts with which your heart can bow before God, waiting on Him to make them living and true in your experience.

Begin this day with the word:

"Unto Thee, O Lord, do I lift up my soul." Bow before Him in stillness, believing that He looks on you and will reveal His presence.

"My soul thirsteth for God, for the living God."

## Confessing Sin

Too often confession of sin is superficial, and sometimes it is neglected. Few Christians realize how necessary it is to be in earnest about the matter, or feel that an honest confession of sin gives power to live the life of victory over sin. In fellowship with the Lord Jesus we need to confess with a sincere heart every sin that may be a hindrance in our Christian lives.

Listen to what David says, "I acknowledged my sin unto Thee; I said, I will confess my transgression, and Thou forgavest the iniquity of my sin. Thou art my hiding-place; Thou shalt compass me about with songs of deliverance" (Ps 32:5-7). David speaks of a time when he was unwilling to confess his sin. "When I kept silence,

Thy hand was heavy upon me." But when he had confessed his sin, a wonderful change came.

Confession means not only that I confess my sin with shame, but that I hand it over to God, trusting Him to take it away. Such a confession implies that I am wholly unable to get rid of my guilt, but by an act of faith I believe God can deliver me. This deliverance means in the first place that I know my sins are forgiven, and secondly, that Christ undertakes to cleanse me from the sin, and keep me from its power.

O Christian, if you desire to have fellowship with Jesus, do not fear to confess each sin in the confident assurance that there is deliverance. Let there be a mutual understanding between the Lord Jesus and yourself that you will confess each sin, and obtain forgiveness. Then you will know your Lord as Jesus Who saves His people from their sin. Believe that there is great power in the confession of sin, for the burden of sin is borne by our Lord and Savior.

## Loving God

In Rev. 1:2-3, eight signs are mentioned showing the zeal and activity of the Church at Ephesus. But there was one bad sign, and the Lord said: "Except thou repent, I will come unto thee, and will remove thy candlestick out of his place." And what was this sign? "Thou hast left thy first love."

We find the same lack in the Church of the present day. There is zeal for the truth, there is continuous and persevering labor, but that which the Lord values most is lacking—tender, fervent love for Himself.

This is a thought of great significance—a church or a community, or a Christian, may be an example in every good work, and yet—the tender love for the Lord Jesus is missing. Consequently there is no personal daily fellowship with Christ, and all the activities with which people satisfy themselves, are nothing in the eyes of the Master Himself.

Dear brother and sister, this book speaks of the fellowship of love with Christ alone. Everything depends on this. Christ came from heaven to love us with the love wherewith the Father loved Him. He suffered and died to win our hearts for this love. His love can be satisfied with nothing less than a deep, personal love on our part.

Christ considers this of the first importance. Let us do so too. Many ministers and missionaries and Christian workers confess with shame that in spite of all their zeal in the Lord's work, their prayer life is defective because they have left their first love. I pray you, write this down on a piece of paper, and remember it continually: the love of Jesus must be all—in my communion with Him, in my work, in all my daily life.

## Shunning the World

John teaches us clearly what he means by the world. He says: "All that is in the world, the lust of the flesh, and the lust of the eyes, and the pride of life, is not of the Father, but is of the world" (1 John 2:16).

The world is the power under which man has fallen through sin. And the god of this world, in order to deceive man, conceals himself under the form of what God has created. The world with its pleasures surrounds the Christian each day with temptations.

This was the case with Eve in the Garden of Eden. We find in Genesis 3 the three characteristics which John mentions: 1. The lust of the flesh—"The woman saw the tree that it was good for food." 2. The lust of the eyes—"It was pleasant to the eyes." The world still comes to us offering much to please the fleshly appetites—much that the eye desires, such as riches and beauty and luxury. 3. And the pride of life—when a man imagines he knows and understands everything.

Our life in the world is full of danger, with the allurements of the flesh.

So John tells us: "Love not the world, for then the love of the Father is not in you." And our Lord calls us, as He called His disciples of old, to leave all and follow Him.

Christian, you live in a dangerous world. Hold fast to the Lord Jesus. As He teaches you to shun the world and its attractions, your love will go out to Him in loyal-hearted service. But remember—there must be daily fellowship with Jesus. His love alone can expel the love of the world. Take time to be alone with your Lord.

## Fearing God

The fear of God—these words characterize the religion of the Old Testament, and the foundation which it laid for the more abundant life of the New. "The gift of holy fear" is still the great desire of the child of God, and an essential part of a life that is to make a real impression on the world around. It is one of the great promises of the new covenant in Jeremiah: "I will make an everlasting covenant with them; and I will put My fear in their hearts, that they shall not depart from Me."

We find the perfect combination of the two in the Acts (9:31): "The churches had peace, being edified, and walking in the fear of the Lord, and in the comfort of the Holy Ghost, were multiplied." And Paul more than once gives fear a high place in the Christian life. "Work out your own salvation with fear and trembling, for it is God that worketh in 'you." "Perfecting holiness in the fear of God" (2 Cor. 7:1).

It has been said that lack of fear of God is one of the things in which our modern times cannot compare favorably with the times of the Puritans and the Covenanters. No wonder then that there is so much cause of complaint in regard to the reading of God's Word, of the worship of His House, and the absence of that spirit of continuous prayer which marked the early Church. Young converts should be fully instructed in the need and the blessedness of a deep fear of God, leading to prayerfulness as one of the essential elements of the life of faith.

Let us earnestly cultivate this grace. Let us hear the word coming out of the very heavens:

"Who shall not fear Thee, O Lord, and glorify Thy name? for Thou only art holy."

"Let us have grace whereby we may serve God acceptably with reverence and godly fear."

As we take the word, "Blessed is the man that feareth the Lord," into our hearts, we shall desire to "Serve the Lord with fear, and rejoice with trembling."

## Submitting to God
Alone with God and wholly for God. May we desire grace from God to learn their deep significance.

As we find that it is not easy to persevere in this being "alone with God," we begin to realize that it is because we are not "wholly for God." God has a right to demand that He should have us completely for Himself. Without this surrender He cannot make His power known. We read in the Old Testament that His servants, Abraham, Moses, Elijah, and David, gave themselves unreservedly to God, so that He could work out His plans through them. It is only the fully surrendered heart that can trust God for all He has promised.

Nature teaches us that if anyone desires to do a great work he must give himself to it. This law is especially true of the love of a mother for her child. She gives herself wholly to the little one whom she loves. And shall we not think it reasonable that the great God of Love should have us wholly for Himself? And shall we not take the watchword, wholly for God, as the keynote for our devotions, every moring as we rise?

Let us meditate on this alone with God, and earnestly ask Him by His almighty power to work in us all that is pleasing in His sight.

"They sought Him with their whole desire, and He was found of them" (2 Chron. 15:15).

"With my whole heart have I sought Thee" (Ps. 119:10).

### Pleasing God

The will is the royal faculty of the soul; it rules over the whole man. Many people become the slaves of sin because they do not decide with a firm will to listen to the voice of conscience. Many Christians make no advance in the prayer life because they have not the courage to say with a strong purpose of will: "By God's help I will do all that God's Word and my own conscience tell me to do. I will make time for prayer and quiet fellowship with Him."

In the practice of prayer it is quite indispensable to say in regard to wandering thoughts, or the brevity and haste of our prayers, or their formality and superficiality, "I will not give way to these things, I will call upon God with all my heart and strength."

This is not easy. One must face the position calmly and decide to go on praying even without zeal or earnestness, "In the few minutes that I spend with God and His Word I am determined to give the time with an undivided heart." Keep on, even though you find it difficult. It will be easier each time you say to God: "Lord, I can be satisfied with nothing less; I seek Thee with my whole heart."

All Judah sought the Lord with their whole desire (or will). God is longing to bless you, but is unable to do so as long as you are not willing to give yourself unreservedly, and with all the strength of your will, to let Him work out His will in you. Speak it out in God's Presence: "Father, I will seek Thee with all my heart and will."

# 5
# Food for Spiritual Growth: Storing God's Word in Our Hearts

"In His Word God speaks to me. In prayer I speak to God."
The interaction between God's Word and our prayer is an
important emphasis in this section. In addition to
expanding on the idea of the Word and prayer being
inseparable and indispensable, Dr. Murray also suggests
the attitude of mind and heart with which we should
approach God's Word.

## Partaking of God's Word

The illustration that our Lord uses, in which the Word of God is compared to our daily bread, is most instructive.

*Bread is indispensable to life.* We all understand this. However strong a person may be, if he takes no nourishment, he will grow weaker, and life will become extinct. Even so with the Word of God. It works powerfully in them that believe.

*Bread must be eaten.* I may know all about bread. I may have bread, and may give it to others. I may have bread in my house and on my table in great abundance, but if through illness I am unable to eat it, I shall die. And so a mere knowledge of God's Word and even the preaching of it to others will not avail me. It is not enough to think about it, I must feed on God's Word, and take it into my heart and life. In love and obedience I must appropriate the words of God, and let them take full possession of my heart. Then they will indeed be words of life.

*Bread must be eaten daily.* And the same is true of God's Word. The Psalmist says: "Blessed is the man whose delight is in the law of the Lord; and in His law doth he meditate day and night." "O how I love Thy law; it is my meditation all the day." Reading God's Word every day is indispensable to secure a strong spiritual life.

When on earth the Lord Jesus learned and obeyed the word of the Father. And if you seek fellowship with Him, you will find Him in His Word. Christ will teach you to commune with the Father, through the Word, even as He did. You will learn, as He did, to live solely for the glory of God and the fulfillment of His Word.

## Studying the Word

*Read God's Word with great reverence.* Meditate a moment in silence on the thought that the words come from God Himself. Bow in deep reverence. Be silent before God and let Him reveal His Word in your heart.

*Read with careful attention.* If you read the words carelessly, thinking that you can grasp their meaning with your human understanding, you will use the words superficially, and not enter into their depths. When one tries to explain anything wonderful or beautiful to us, we give our entire attention to try to understand what is said. How much higher and deeper are God's thoughts than our thoughts. "As the heaven is higher than the earth, so are My thoughts higher than your thoughts." We need to give our undivided attention to understand even the superficial meaning of the words. How much harder to grasp the spiritual meaning?

*Read expecting the guidance of God's Spirit.* It is God's
Spirit alone that can make the Word a living power in
our hearts and lives. Read Psalm 119. Notice how earnestly David prays that God will teach him, and open his
eyes, and give him understanding, and incline his heart
to God's ways. As you read, remember that God's Word
and God's Spirit are inseparable.

*Read with the firm purpose of keeping the Word in your
heart and in your life at all times.* The whole heart and the
whole life must come under the influence of the Word.
David said: "O how I love Thy law; it is my meditation
all the day." And so in the midst of his daily work, the
believer can cherish God's Word in his heart, and meditate on it. Read Psalm 119 again, until you accept God's
Word with all your heart, and pray that God may teach
you to understand it, and to carry out its precepts in
your life.

## Using the Word

Reading God's Word and praying are both indispensable and should not be separated in our communion
with God. In His Word God speaks to me; in prayer, I
speak to God.

The Word teaches me to know the God to whom I
pray; it teaches me how to pray. It gives me precious
promises to encourage me in prayer. It often gives me
answers to prayer.

The Word comes from God's heart and brings His
thoughts and His love into my heart. And then in
prayer, the Word goes back from my heart into His
great heart of love.

The Word teaches me God's will—His promises of
what He will do for me, as food for my faith, and also

the will of His commands, to which I surrender myself in loving obedience.

The more I pray, the more I feel my need of the Word, and rejoice in it. The more I read God's Word, the more I have to pray about, and the more power I have in prayer. One great cause of prayerlessness is that we read God's Word too little, or only superficially.

It is the Holy Spirit through whom the Word has been spoken who is also the Spirit of prayer. He will teach me how to receive the Word, and how to approach God.

How blessed would it be, what a power and an inspiration in our worship, if we took God's Word as from Himself, turning it into prayer, and definitely expecting an answer. It is the secret of God's presence, that by the Holy Spirit God's Word will become our delight and our strength.

God's Word in deepest reverence in our hearts, and on our lips, and in our lives, will be a never failing fountain of strength and blessing.

Let us believe that God's Word is full of a quickening power that will make us strong, ready to expect and receive great things from God. Above all, it will give us the daily blessed fellowship with the living God.

"Blessed is the man whose delight is in the law of the Lord; in His law doth he meditate day and night" (Ps. 1:2).

# 6
# Person to Person with God

If you use the telephone frequently, you may want to keep track of how much time you spend talking during a day or week and compare with your time for prayer. Then review on these pages the various needs for which Christians should pray. These, and the scriptural "calls to prayer" interwoven, make clear the Christian responsibility to the work of prayer—and the blessings derived from it.

**Praying in Private**

Have you ever thought what a wonderful privilege it is that on any day and in any hour we have the liberty of asking God to meet us, and to hear what He has to say? We would imagine that every Christian use such a privilege gladly and faithfully.

"When thou prayest," says Jesus "enter into thine inner chamber, and having shut thy door, pray to thy Father which is in secret." That means two things. Shut the world out, withdraw from all worldly thoughts and occupations, and shut yourself in alone with God, to pray to Him in secret. Let this be your chief object in prayer, to realize the presence of your heavenly Father. Let your watchword be: Alone with God.

This is only the beginning. I must take time to realize His presence with me, and pray to my Father in the full assurance that He knows how I long for His help and guidance, and that He will hear me.

Then follows the great promise: "Thy Father which seeth in secret shall reward thee openly." My Father will see to it that my prayer is not in vain. All through the occupations of a busy day, the answer to my prayer will be granted. Prayer in secret will be followed by the secret working of God in my heart.

As the Lord Jesus has given us the promise of His presence, and shows us the way to the quiet place, He will teach us to pray. It is through Him that we have access to the Father. Be childlike and trusting in your fellowship with Christ. Confess each sin, bring your every need. Offer your prayer to the Father in the name of Christ. Prayer in fellowship with Jesus cannot be in vain.

## Persevering Prayer

One of the greatest drawbacks to the life of prayer is the fact that the answer does not come as speedily as we expect. We are discouraged by the thought: "Perhaps I do not pray aright," and so we do not persevere in prayer. This was a lesson that our Lord taught often and urgently. If we consider the matter we can see that there may be a reason for the delay, and the waiting may bring a blessing to our souls. Our desire must grow deeper and stronger, and we must ask with our whole heart. God puts us into the practicing school of persevering prayer, that our weak faith may be strengthened. Do believe that there is a great blessing in the delayed answer to prayer.

Above all, God draws us into closer fellowship with Himself. When our prayers are not answered, we learn to realize that the fellowship and nearness and love of God are more to us than the answers to our petitions, and we continue in prayer. What a blessing Jacob received through the delay in the answer to his prayer! He saw God face to face, and as a prince he had power with God and prevailed.

Christians, listen to this warning. Be not impatient or discouraged if the answer does not come. "Continue in prayer." "Pray without ceasing." You will find it an unspeakable blessing to do so. You will ask whether your prayer is really in accordance with the will of God, and the Word of God. You will inquire if it is in the right spirit and in the Name of Christ. Keep on praying. You will learn that the delay in the answer to prayer is one of the most precious means of grace that God can bestow on you. You will learn too that those who have persevered often and long before God, in pleading His promises, are those who have had the greatest power with God in prayer.

## Interceding for Individuals

In our body every member has its place and function. This is true also in society and in the Church. Every member should aim for the welfare of the whole group.

In the Church the thought is found too often that the salvation of men is the work of the minister; whereas he generally deals with the crowd, and seldom on an individual basis. The believer does not understand that it is necessary for him to testify to those around him—for the nourishment and the strengthening of his own spiritual life, and for the ingathering of souls. Unconverted souls suffer unspeakable loss because Christ is not personally introduced to them by each believer they meet.

The thought of intercession for those around us is too
seldom found. Restoring it to a right place in the Christian life would mean much to the Church and its missions!

When will Christians learn the great truth that what
God in heaven desires to do needs prayer on earth as its
indispensable condition. As we realize this we see that
intercession is the chief element in the conversion of
souls. All our efforts are vain, without the power of the
Holy Spirit given in answer to prayer. It is when ministers and people unite in a covenant of prayer and testimony that the Church will flourish, and that every
believer will understand the part he is to take.

And what can we do to stir up the spirit of intercession? There is a two-fold answer. Let every Christian, as
he begins to get an insight into the need and the power
of intercession, begin to exercise it on behalf of single
individuals. Pray for your children, for your relatives
and friends, for all with whom God brings you into con-
tact. If you feel that you do not have the power to intercede, let the discovery humble you and drive you to the
mercy seat. God wants every redeemed child of His to
intercede for the perishing. It is the vital breath of the
normal Christian life—the proof that it is born from
above.

Then pray intensely and persistently that God will
give the power of His Holy Spirit to you and His children around you, that the power of intercession will
have the place that God will honor.

## Praying for Believers

"With *all* prayer and supplication praying at *all* seasons,
watching thereunto in *all* perseverance and *all* supplication" (Eph. 6:18, *R.V.*). Notice how Paul repeats the

words in the intensity of his desire to reach the hearts of his readers. It is, "all prayer, all seasons, all perseverance, all supplication."

Paul felt so deeply the unity of the Body of Christ, and he was so sure that that unity could only be realized in the exercise of love and prayer, that he pleaded with the believers at Ephesus to pray for all saints, not only in their immediate circle, but in all the Church of Christ. "Unity is strength." As we exercise this power of intercession with perseverance, we shall be delivered from self with all its feeble prayers, and lifted up to that enlargement of heart in which the love of Christ can flow freely and fully through us.

Believers often are too occupied with themselves, and with what God must do for them. Let us realize that we have here a call to every believer to give himself without ceasing to the exercise of love and prayer. It is as we forget ourselves, believing that God will take charge of us, and yield ourselves to the great work of calling down the blessing of God on our brethren, that the whole Church will be fitted to do its work in making Christ known to every creature. This alone is the healthy and blessed life of a child of God who has yielded himself to Christ Jesus.

Pray for God's children and the Church around you. Pray for all the work in which they are engaged, or ought to be. Pray at all seasons in the Spirit for all God's saints. There is no blessedness greater than that of abiding communion with God. And there is no way that leads to the enjoyment of this more surely than the life of intercession for which these words of Paul appeal.

## Interceding for Laborers

"The harvest truly is plenteous, but the laborers are few;

pray ye therefore the Lord of the harvest, that He will send forth laborers into His harvest" (Matt. 9:37, 38). The disciples understood very little of what these words meant. Christ gave them as a seed-thought, to be lodged in their hearts for later use. At Pentecost, as they saw how many of the new converts were ready in the power of the Spirit to testify of Christ, they must have realized how the ten days of continuous united prayer had brought this blessing too, as the fruit of the Spirit's power.

Christ meant to teach us that, however large the field may be, and however few the laborers, prayer is the best, the sure, the only means of supplying the need.

What we must understand is that it is not only in time of need that the prayer must be sent up, but that the whole work is to be carried on in the spirit of prayer, so that the prayer for laborers will be in perfect harmony with the whole of our life and effort.

In the China Inland Mission, when the number of missionaries had gone up to 200, a Conference felt so deeply the need of more laborers for districts unprovided for, that after much prayer they asked God to give them within a year 100 additional laborers and 10,000 pounds to meet the expenses. They agreed to continue in prayer day by day throughout the year. At the end of the time the 100 suitable men and women had been found, and 11,000 pounds.

The meet the needs of the world, its open fields, and its waiting souls, the churches all complain of the lack of laborers and of funds. Does not Christ's voice call us to the united and unceasing prayer of the first disciples? God is faithful, by the power of His Spirit, to supply every need. Let the Church take the posture of united prayer. God hears.

## Interceding for Missions

How to multiply the number of Christians, who will intercede for the conversion of men? That is the supreme question of Foreign Missions. Every other consideration is secondary to that of wielding the torches of prayer.

That those who love this work will pray unceasingly for its triumph, we take for granted. To such, not only the morning watch and the hours of stated devotion, but all times and seasons witness an attitude of intercession that refuses to let God go until He crowns His workers with victory.

Missions have their root in the love of Christ. As men are so earnest in seeking to carry out God's plans for the natural world, so God's children should be at least as wholehearted in seeking to bring Christ's love to all mankind. Intercession is the chief means appointed by God to bring the great redemption within reach of all.

Pray for the missionaries, that the Christ-life may be clear and strong, that they may be men of prayer and filled with love, showing forth the power of the spiritual life.

Pray for the native Christians, that they may know the glory of the mystery among the heathen, Christ in them the hope of glory.

Pray for the instruction classes, and all the pupils in schools, that the teaching of God's Word may be in power. Pray specially for the native pastors and evangelists, that the Holy Spirit may fill them to be witnesses for Christ among their countrymen.

Pray, above all, for the Church of Christ, that it may be lifted out of its indifference, and that every believer may be brought to understand that the one object of his life is to help to make Christ King on the earth.

## Praying for a Lost World

This earth, now under the power of the Evil One, will one day be renewed and filled with the glory of God—a new earth wherein righteousness dwells. What a prospect! Though we believe it so little, it will surely come to pass. God's Word pledges it. God's Son by His blood and death conquered the power of sin, and through the Eternal Spirit the power of God is working out His purpose.

But what a great and difficult work. It is near two thousand years since Christ gave the promise and ascended the throne, and yet more than one-half of the human race have never learned to know even the name of Jesus. And of the other half, what millions are called by His name, yet do not know Him. This great work of bringing the knowledge of Christ to every creature has been entrusted to a Church that thinks little of her responsibility and of the consequence of her neglect. We may indeed ask: Will the work ever be done? Blessed be His name! His power and His faithfulness are pledges that one day we shall see the whole earth filled with the glory of God.

O that Christian people might understand that the extension of God's Kingdom can only be affected by the united and continuing prayer of men and women who wait upon Christ in the assurance that what they desire He will do for them!

My reader, do become one of those intercessors who really believe that in answer to your prayer the crucified Jesus will do far more than you can ask or think.

## Growing Through Prayer

There is nothing that can bring us nearer to God, and lead us deeper into His love than the work of intercession.

Nothing can so closely link us to Jesus Christ, the great Intercessor, and give us the experience of His power and Spirit resting on us, as the yielding of our lives to the work of bringing the redemption to our fellow men. There is nothing in which we shall know more of the powerful working of the Holy Spirit than in the prayer breathed by Him into our hearts, "Abba, Father," in all the meaning that it had for Christ in Gethsemane. There is nothing that can so help us to prove the power and the faithfulness of God to His Word, as when we reach out in intercession for the multitudes, either in the Church or in the darkness of heathenism. As we pour out our souls as a living sacrifice before God, with the one persistent plea that He will open the windows of heaven and send down His abundant blessing, God will be glorified, our souls will reach their highest destiny, and God's Kingdom will come.

It will help us to understand and to experience the living unity of the Body of Christ, and the irresistible power that it can exert, as the daily and continuing fellowship with God's children in the persistent plea that God will have mercy upon Zion, and make her a light to those sitting in darkness.

How little we realize what we are losing in not living in fervent intercession! What we can gain for ourselves and for the world if we allow God's Spirit to master our whole being!

In heaven Christ prays. His whole intercourse with His Father is prayer; an asking and receiving of the fullness of the Spirit for His people. God delights in nothing so much as in prayer. Shall we not learn to believe that the highest blessings of heaven will be unfolded to us as we pray more?

# 7
# The Spirit-Filled Life: No Power Shortage Here

While the world is having to come to grips with shortages of key commodities, Christians have an abundant resource in the Holy Spirit. Christ referred to the Holy Spirit who was to come as Living Water springing up to eternal life and flowing out. How graphically this describes the multiple work of the Holy Spirit—first within the believer to bless him and then to bring life and blessing to others.

## The Coming of the Holy Spirit

Our Lord, on the last night that He was with His disciples, promised to send the Holy Spirit as a Comforter. Although His bodily presence was removed, they would realize His presence with them in a wonderful way. The Holy Spirit as God would so reveal Christ in their hearts that they would experience His presence with them continually. The Spirit would glorify Christ and would reveal Him in heavenly love and power.

How little Christians understand and believe and experience this truth. We fail in our duty as ministers if in a little book like this, or in our preaching, we encourage Christians to love the Lord Jesus, without at the same time warning them that they cannot do this in their own strength. God, the Holy Spirit, will shed abroad His love in our hearts, and teach us to love Him fervently.

Through the Holy Spirit we may experience the love and abiding presence of the Lord Jesus all the day.

But let us remember that the Spirit of God must have entire possession of us. He claims our whole heart and life. He will strengthen us in the inner man, so that we have fellowship with Christ, keep His commandments, and abide in His love.

When once we have grasped this truth, we will begin to feel our deep dependence on the Holy Spirit, and pray the Father to send Him in power into our hearts. The Spirit will teach us to love the Word, to meditate on it and to keep it. He will reveal the love of Christ to us, that we may love Him. Then we shall see that life in the love of Christ is a blessed reality.

## Waiting for the Holy Spirit

After our Lord had given the great command: "Go into all the world and preach the Gospel to every creature," He again added another: "Tarry till ye be endued with power from on high." "Wait for the promise of the Father." "Ye shall be baptized with the Holy Ghost not many days hence."

All Christians agree that the great command to preach the Gospel to every creature was not only for the disciples, but is binding on us too. All, however, do not appear to consider that the very last command, not to preach until they had received the power from on high, is equally binding on us as it was on the disciples. The Church appears to have lost possession of that which ought to be to her a secret of secrets—the abiding consciousness, day by day, that it is only as she lives in the power of the Holy Spirit that she can preach the Gospel in power. This is why there is so much preaching and working with so little result. It goes back to the universal complaint that there is insufficient prayer to empower the Church.

In this book we desire to study the secret of Pentecost as it is to be found in the words and the deeds of our blessed Master, and in the words and the deeds of His disciples as they took Him at His word, and continued with one accord in prayer and supplication, until the promise was fulfilled. They became full of the Holy Spirit, and proved what the mighty power of their God could do through them.

Let us earnestly seek the grace of the Holy Spirit, who can reveal to us what eye hath not not seen, nor ear heard, nor hath entered into the heart of man to conceive—the things which God hath done and loves to do for them that wait upon Him. Let us pray that the lost secret may be found—the sure promise that in answer to fervent prayer the power of the Holy Spirit will be given.

## Power From on High

The Lord had said to the disciples: "Without Me ye can do nothing." Why is it then that He chose these impotent, helpless men to send them out to conquer the world for Him? It was that in their feebleness they might yield themselves and give Him as Lord the opportunity to show His power working through them. As the Father had done all the work in Christ when He was upon earth, so Christ in heaven would now be the Great Worker, proving in them that all power had been given to Him in heaven and on earth. Their place would be to pray, to believe, and to yield themselves to the mighty power of Christ.

The Holy Spirit would not be in them as a power which they could possess. But He would possess them, and their work would be the work of the Almighty Christ. Their posture each day would be that of dependence and prayer, and of confident expectation.

The Apostles had learned to know Christ intimately. They had seen all His mighty works; they had received His teaching; they had gone with Him through all His sufferings, even to the death of the cross. And they had not only seen Him but known Him in the power of His resurrection and the experience of that resurrection life in their own hearts. Yet they were not capable of making Him known aright, until He Himself had taken possession of them by His Spirit dwelling in them.

Everything calls the Christian to rest content with nothing less than the indwelling life and power of the Holy Spirit. Nothing less than having Christ speaking through us in the power of His omnipotence will make us able witnesses of the New Testament, bringing salvation to them that hear us.

## Made Holy

"And the God of peace Himself sanctify you wholly; and may your spirit and soul and body be preserved entire, without blame at the coming of our Lord Jesus Christ. Faithful is He that calleth you, Who will also do it" (Thess. 5:23, 24, R.V.).

What a promise! One would expect to see all God's children clinging to it, claiming its fulfilment, but unbelief does not know what to think of it, and but few count it their treasure and joy.

Just listen. The God of peace—the peace He made by the blood of the cross, the peace that passeth all understanding, keeping our hearts and thoughts in Christ Jesus—none other but Himself can and will do it. This God of peace Himself promises to sanctify us. It is God who is doing the work. It is in personal fellowship with God that we become holy.

Ought not each of us to rejoice with exceeding joy at the prospect? But it is as if the promise is too great, and so it is repeated and amplified. May your spirit—the inmost part of our being, created for fellowship with God—and your soul, the seat of life and all its powers—and body, through which sin entered, in which sin proved its power even unto death, but which has been redeemed in Christ: spirit, soul, and body be preserved entire, without blame, at the coming of our Lord Jesus Christ.

To prevent the possibility of any misconception, as if it is too great to be literally true, the words are added: "Faithful is He that calleth you, who will also do it." Yes, He has said: "I the Lord have spoken it; and I, in Christ and through the Holy Spirit, will do it." All that He asks is that we come and abide in close fellowship with Himself every day. As the heat of the sun shines on the body and warms it, the fire of His holiness will burn in us, and make us holy. Child of God, beware of unbelief. It dishonors God, it robs your soul of its heritage. Take refuge in the word: "Faithful is He that calleth you, Who will also do it." Let every thought of your calling wake the response: "Faithful is He that calleth you, Who will also do it."

**Set Apart**
In the Old Testament God was revealed as the Thrice Holy One. The Spirit is mentioned more than a

hundred times, but only three times as the Holy Spirit. In the New Testament the word "Holy" is ascribed to the Holy Spirit, and Christ sanctified Himself for us, that we might be holy. The great work of the Holy Spirit is to glorify Christ in us as our sanctification.

Has this truth ever taken hold of you—at group prayer meetings or in your private devotions—that the great object for which the Holy Spirit is given is to sanctify you? If you do not accept this truth, the Holy Spirit cannot do His purifying work. If you only want the Spirit to help you to be a little better, and to pray a little more, you will not get very far. But when you once understand that He has the name of Holy Spirit in order definitely to impart God's holiness, and will sanctify you, then you will begin to realize that the Holy Spirit dwells in your heart.

And what will be the result? You will feel that He must rule and control each day. All of life and conversation must be in the Spirit. My prayer, my faith, my fellowship with the Father, and all my work in God's service, must be completely under His sway. As the Spirit of holiness, He is the Spirit of my sanctification.

Dear brother, what I have said is deep, eternal truth. Even if we are willing to accept this truth, and meditate on it daily, it will be of no avail if we do not wait upon God to grant us the Spirit of heavenly wisdom, and a vision of what God has intended for us in His wonderful gift—the Spirit of sanctification. Each morning say slowly and calmly: "Abba, Father, for this new day renew within me the gift of Thy Holy Spirit."

## Our Body His Temple
What does the Spirit expect of me? Your body is His

temple. The temple of God is holy, devoted to His service. You are not your own and have no right to please yourself. You have been bought with the blood of Christ. The Spirit has absolute right to your whole life. Therefore you must glorify God in your body and your spirit, which are God's. The Holy Spirit is the Spirit of God's holiness; He comes to make me holy and expects me to obey Him fully.

Let me dwell upon these words that I may comprehend clearly the relationship between the Spirit and me, and what He expects of me. He asks that I, as one dearly bought with the blood of Christ, and no longer my own, shall will to please Him in all things and to follow His leading. All that I owe to God, and to the Lord Jesus, must be shown in my conduct towards the Holy Spirit. I must be guided by Him. He expects me to say each morning, "Speak, Lord, Thy servant heareth, I yield myself to obey the prompting of Thy voice within me." He expects absolute obedience.

Furthermore He wants me to keep in close touch with Him by taking time each day to renew the bond between Him and me. My whole life must be yielded to Him, that it will bear His glorious fruits.

He also expects that in His strength I shall witness for Jesus Christ, and consider it my work to help to bring souls to the Lord Jesus. The Spirit expects that my body shall be a temple of God from which praise to God the Father and His Son Jesus Christ will arise.

## Living Water

Our Lord, in His conversation with the Samaritan woman, said: "The water that I shall give him shall be in him a well of water springing up to eternal life." In our text the promise is even greater: rivers of living waters flowing from him, bringing life and blessing to others. John says further that this refers to the Holy Spirit, who should come when Christ had been glorified, for the Holy Spirit was not yet poured out. The Spirit of God was mentioned in the Old Testament, but the Holy Spirit had not yet been given. Christ must first be offered through the eternal Spirit (on the cross) (Heb. 9:14), and raised from the dead by the spirit of holiness (Rom. 1:4), and receive from the Father power to send forth the Holy Spirit. Then only would the Christian be able to say: Now the Holy Spirit of Christ is in me.

What do we need in order to experience the promise of the living water? The inner attachment to Christ, the unreserved surrender to fellowship with Him, and the firm assurance that His Spirit will work in us what we cannot do. In one word: He that believeth on Me. We need a faith that rejoices in the divine love, and depends on Him day by day to grant us grace that living water may flow from us.

If the water from a reservoir is to flow into a house all day, one thing is necessary—the connection must be perfect. Then the water passes through the pipe of its own accord. So the union between you and Christ must be uninterrupted; your faith must accept Christ and depend on Him to sustain the new life.

Let your faith rejoice that Jesus Christ gives us the Holy Spirit, and may you have the assurance that the Holy Spirit is within you as a fountain of blessing.

## Rejoicing in the Spirit

A Christian man said to me, shortly after his conversion: "I always thought that if I became religious it would be impossible for me to do my worldly business. The two things seemed so contrary. I felt like I was trying to dig a vineyard with a bag of sand on my shoulders. But when I found the Lord, I was so filled with joy that I could do my work cheerfully from morning till night. The bag of sand was gone; the joy of the Lord was my strength for all my work."

Truly a significant lesson. Many Christians do not understand that the joy of the Lord will keep them and fit them for their work. Even slaves, when filled with the love of Christ, could testify to the happiness that He gave.

Read Romans 14:17 and see how the kingdom of God is pure joy and peace through the Holy Spirit, and how God will "fill us with all joy and peace in believing," "through the power of the Holy Ghost." Then try to realize that the Holy Spirit will give this joy and peace of Christ in our hearts. To many the thought of the Holy Spirit is a matter of grief and self-reproach, of desire and disappointment, of something too high and holy for them. What a foolish thought, that the great gift of the Father, meant to keep us in the joy and peace of Christ should be a matter of self-reproach and care.

Remember Galatians 5:22, and listen attentively to the voice of the Spirit each day as He points to Jesus Christ, who offers you this wonderful fruit: "My Love, My Joy, My Peace." "On whom, though now ye see Him not, yet believing, ye rejoice greatly with joy unspeakable and full of glory" (1 Pet. 1:8). Pray in all humility to the Holy Spirit, believing firmly that He will lead you into the joy of the Lord.

# 8
# Keeping on Course: Allowing the Navigator to Chart Our Way

In this segment Dr. Murray refers to the Holy Spirit as the Divine Leader who enables us to abide in Christ and to walk the Christ life IF we regard our old nature as crucified with Christ. Where "the flesh" is allowed to have its way, the Spirit cannot exercise power, Dr. Murray emphasizes. He questions whether this truth has been sufficiently taught. Or is it that we are unwilling to deny self?

## The Old Nature Crucified

Paul teaches, "In me, that is, in my flesh, dwelleth no good thing." (Rom. 7:18). And again "The mind of the flesh is enmity against God; for it is not subject to the law of God, neither indeed can it be" (Rom. 8:7). When Adam lost the Spirit of God, he became flesh. Flesh is the corrupt nature that we inherit from Adam. Paul also wrote, "Our old man was crucified with Him" (Rom. 6:6). And again, "They that are in Christ Jesus have crucified the flesh."

When the disciples heard and obeyed the call of Jesus to follow Him, they honestly meant to do so, but as He later taught them what that would invoke, they were far from being ready to obey. Those who are Christ's and have accepted Him as the Crucified One little understand what that includes. By that act of surrender they actually have crucified the flesh, and consented to re-gard it as an accursed thing, nailed to the cross of Christ.

How many there are who have never thought of this. It may be that the preaching of Christ crucified has been defective in that the truth of our being crucified with Christ has not been taught. They shrink back from the self-denial that it implies, and as a result, where the flesh is allowed to have its way, the Spirit of Christ cannot exert His power.

Paul taught the Galatians: "Walk in the Spirit, and ye shall not fulfill the lusts of the flesh." "As many as are led by the Spirit of God, they are the children of God." And the Spirit alone can guide us as the flesh is kept in the place of crucifixion.

Blessed Lord, how little I understood when I accepted Thee in faith that I crucified once for all the flesh with its passions and lusts! Teach me, I pray, to believe and so to live in Thee, the Crucified One.

## The Christ Life

Christ's life was more than His teaching, more than His work, more even than His death. It was His life in the sight of God and man that gave value to what He said and did and suffered. And it is this life, glorified in the resurrection, that He imparts to His people, and enables them to live out before men.

"Hereby shall all men know that ye are My disciples, if ye love one another." It was the life in the new brother-hood of the Holy Spirit that made both Jews and Greeks feel that there was some super-human power about Christ's disciples; they gave living proof of the truth of what they said, that God's love had come down and taken possession of them.

It has often been said of the missionary, that unless he lives on an entirely different level from that on which other men live, he misses the deepest secret of power and success in his work. When Christ sent His disciples forth, it was with the command: "Tarry till ye be endued with power from on high." "Wait, and ye shall receive the power of the Holy Ghost, and be My witnesses to the ends of the earth." Many a missionary has felt that it is not learning and not zeal, and not the willingness for self-sacrifice in Christ's service, but the secret experience of the life hid with Christ in God, that enables him to meet and overcome every difficulty.

Everything depends upon the life with God in Christ being right. It was so with Christ, with the disciples, with Paul. It is the simplicity and intensity of our life in Christ Jesus, and of the life of Christ Jesus in us, that sustains a man in the daily drudgery of work, that makes him conquer self and everything that hinders the Christ life, and gives the victory over the powers of evil, and over the hearts from which the evil spirits have to be cast out.

The life is everything. It was so in Christ Jesus. It must be so in His servants. It can be so, because Christ Himself will live in us. When He spoke the word, "Lo, I am with you alway," He meant nothing less than this: Every day I am with you, the secret of your life, your joy, and your strength.

## Walking in the Spirit

The word "walk" reminds us of daily life with our fellow men. The Christian in his walk and conversation must follow the leading of the Spirit. This is the sign of the spiritual man, who does not trust in the flesh.

People speak as though the Spirit were only needed in

our intercourse with God when we pray, or for our work in the service of the Kingdom. This is a great mistake. God gives us His Spirit for the whole day. We need Him most in the midst of our daily work because the world has such power to lead us away from God. We need to pray to the Father every morning for a fresh portion of His Spirit. During the course of the day let us remind ourselves that the Spirit is with us, and lift up our hearts to God, remembering that the Spirit abides with us always.

Paul says: "As ye have received Christ Jesus our Lord, so walk ye in Him"; and again: "Put on the Lord Jesus Christ." As I put on my cloak when I go out, so the Christian must put on the Lord Jesus, and show by his conduct that Christ lives in him, and that he walks by the Spirit.

"Walk in the Spirit, and ye shall not fulfil the lusts of the flesh." As long as we are not under the guidance of The Holy Spirit, the flesh will rule over us. Oh that we knew the unspeakable value of the grace that God has given! The Spirit of His Son in our hearts will cry "Abba, Father," so that we may walk the whole day in God's presence as His beloved children. Christian, learn this lesson: you may walk by the Spirit at all times. Thank God continually for this Divine Leader, who gives us daily renewal from heaven, and enables us to walk and to abide in Christ.

## Obeying God

When God gave Israel the Law, He promised to be their God if they would obey Him. But Israel had no power to keep the law. So God gave them a "new covenant," to enable His people to live a life of obedience. We read

"I will write My law in their hearts" (Jer. 31:33). "I will put My fear in their heart, that they shall not depart from Me" (Jer. 32:40). "I will cause you to walk in My statutes" (Ezk. 36:27). These promises gave the assurance that obedience would be their delight.

Let us listen to what the Lord Jesus says about obedience (John 14:21-23): "He that keepeth My commandments, he it is that loveth Me; and he that loveth Me shall be loved of My Father, and I will love him, and We will make our abode with him." And in John 15:10, "If ye keep My commandments, ye shall abide in My love." These words are an inexhaustible treasure. Faith can firmly trust Christ to enable us to live such a life of love. and of obedience.

No father can train his children unless they are obedient. No teacher can teach a child who continues to disobey him. No general can lead his soldiers to victory without prompt obedience. Pray God to imprint this lesson on your heart: the life of faith is a life of obedience. As Christ lived in obedience to the Father, so we too need obedience for a life in the love of God.

You may say, "I cannot be obedient, it is quite impossible." Yes, impossible to you, but not to God. He has promised "to cause you to walk in His statutes." Pray and meditate on these words, and the Holy Spirit will enlighten your eyes, so that you will have power to do God's will. Let your fellowship with the Father and with the Lord Jesus Christ have as its one aim and object—a life of quiet, determined, unquestioning obedience.

## Stewards of God's Love

A steward is the man to whom the master entrusts his treasures to apportion to those who have a right to them. God in heaven needs men on earth to make known the treasures of His love, and to give them to those who have need. The minister of the Gospel is a steward of the mystery of God, and above all of the deep mystery of His everlasting love, and all the blessings that flow from it.

It is required in stewards that a man be found faithful; he must devote himself wholly to his life task. He must be faithful at his work, and always at his post in the palace or house where the treasures are stored up. So the minister of the Gospel must himself be faithful, living each day in the love and fellowship of God. He must be faithful not only to God, but to his fellow men, caring for the needs of the souls entrusted to him, and ready to recommend God's love, and to share it with others. This divine love is a mystery, and can only dwell in a heart set apart for God and satisfied with His love, which flows from Him as a stream of living water.

O child of God, try to have a deeper insight into what it means to be a steward of the wonderful love of God to sinners. Pray much and often for your ministers that they may be faithful stewards of the mystery of God and His Love.

And you, my beloved brethren, to whom the love of God in heaven, and of Christ on the cross, is entrusted, remember that people are dependent on your faithfulness in living life in fellowship with God. Then you will be able with joy, and in the power of the Holy Spirit, to pass on the love of God to souls who so greatly need it.

## One Day at a Time
It is a step forward in the Christian life when one definitely decides to have fellowship with God in His Word

each day without fail. His perseverance will be crowned with success, if he is in earnest. His experience may be as follows:

On waking in the morning, God will be his first thought. He must set apart a time for prayer, and resolve to give God time to hear his requests, and to reveal Himself to him. Then he may speak out all his desires to God, and expect an answer.

Later in the day, even if only for a few minutes, he will take time to keep up the fellowship with God. And again in the evening a quiet period is necessary to review the day's work, and with confession of sin receive the assurance of forgiveness, and dedicate himself afresh to God and His service.

One will gradually get an insight into what is lacking in his life, and will be ready to say: Not only "every day" but "all the day." He will realize that the Holy Spirit is in him unceasingly, just as his breathing is continuous. He will make it his aim to gain assurance through faith that the Holy Spirit, and the Lord Jesus, and the Father Himself will grant His presence and help all through the day.

The Holy Spirit says: "Today." "Behold, now is the accepted time!" A man who had undergone a serious operation asked his doctor, "How long will I have to lie here?" And the answer came: "Only a day at a time." And that is the law of the Christian life. God gave the manna daily, the morning and evening sacrifice on the altar—by these God showed that His children should live by the day. Seek this day to trust to the leading of the Holy Spirit the whole day. You need not care for the morrow, but rest in the assurance that He who has led you today, will draw still nearer tomorrow.

# 9
# Bearing Fruit:
# For the Glory of God

When Christ talked about the vine and its fruit He mirrored the abundant life of the believer. Just as fruit of the vine benefits the vineyard owner, so the fruitful Christian life pleases God. He didn't thrust us into this role on our own, but abiding in Him—as branches of a vine—we are enabled to bear fruit for His glory.

## Witnessing for Christ

Christ's servants are to be witnesses to Him, testifying of His love, of His power to redeem, of His continual presence, and of His power to work in them.

Without claiming authority or power, without wisdom or eloquence, without influence or position, each is called, not only by his words, but by his life and action, to be a living proof and witness of what Jesus can do.

This is the only weapon Christ's witnesses are to use in bringing persons to the feet of Christ. When the first disciples were filled with the Spirit they began to speak of the mighty things that Christ had done.

It was in this power that those who were scattered abroad by persecution went forth, even as far as Antioch, preaching in the name of Jesus, and a multitude of the heathen believed. They had no commission from the Apostles; they had no special gifts or training, but out of the fullness of the heart they spoke of Jesus Christ. They could not be silent; they were filled with the life and the love of Christ.

It was this that gave the Gospel its power of increase; each new convert became a witness for Christ.

A heathen writer commenting on the persecutions said that if the Christians were only content to keep the worship of Jesus to themselves they would not have to suffer. But in their zeal they wanted Christ to rule over all.

Here we have the secret of a flourishing Church: each believer a witness for Jesus. Because so few are willing in daily life to testify that Jesus is Lord, the Church is weak.

What a call to prayer! Lord, teach Thy disciples the blessedness of so knowing Jesus and the power of His love, that they may find their highest joy in witnessing to who He is and what He has done for them.

## Honoring God

Fruit is that which a tree or a vine yields for the benefit of its owner. All that the Lord Jesus has taught us about His abiding in us and we in Him is to make us understand that it is not for our benefit, but for His good pleasure and the honor of the Father. We, as branches of the Heavenly Vine, receive grace that we may win souls for Him.

Can this be the reason why you have not enjoyed unbroken fellowship with Christ? Have you forgotten that the object of fellowship and communion is to save others? Have you given too much thought to your own sanctification and joy, not remembering that as Christ sought His blessing and glory from the Father in the sacrifice of Himself for us, so we, too, are called to live solely to bring Christ to others? It is for this purpose that we become branches of the Heavenly Vine, in order to continue the work that He began, and with the same wholeheartedness.

When Christ was on earth, He said, "I am the light of the world"; but speaking of the time when He should be taken from the earth He said, "Ye are the light of the world."

How often you have said to the Lord, "I yield myself to Thee for cleansing and keeping and to be made holy," but you have hesitated to add "to be used of Thee in the salvation of others." Let us acknowledge our failure here and humbly offer ourselves to the Lord for His work. Let us begin by praying for those around us, looking for opportunities to help them, and not being satisfied until we bear fruit to the glory of the Father.

Christ said, "Apart from Me ye can do nothing." He knows our weakness. He has promised, "He that abideth in Me beareth much fruit." Let all that we learn of the more abundant life and abounding grace constrain us to win souls for Jesus.

## Living Abundantly

Everyone can understand the difference between life that is weak and sickly, and life that has abundant vitality. St. Paul spoke of the Corinthians as not spiritual but carnal, as young children in Christ incapable of assimilating strong meat, or of understanding the deeper truth of the Gospel (see 1 Cor. 3 and Heb. 5). The majority of Christians never advance beyond first principles. They are dull of hearing and remain carnal Christians. Others, a minority, show forth the abundant riches of grace. All through the history of the Church we find this difference. In our day, too, the number is small of those who seek to live wholly for God, and who, being spiritually minded, have large thoughts of the abundant life there is in Christ. They witness to the glory of Christ "full of grace and truth." "For of His fullness we all received, and grace for grace" (John 1:16).

The preacher's aim should be so to declare the fullness of God's grace in Jesus Christ as to make Christians ashamed of the poverty of their spiritual life, and encourage them to believe that "life abundant" in the Spirit is for them.

Dear reader, ask yourself if you are living the abundant life Jesus came to give you. Is it manifest in your love to the Savior and in the abundant fruit you bear to the glory of God in soul winning? If not, pray God to strengthen your faith that you may abound in every good work. Let Jesus be precious to you. Daily communion with Him is indispensable. He will teach you by His Holy Spirit to honor Him by an abundant life.